Poppies

AMY SEXAUER

Poppies

AMY SEXAUER

Publisher: Dead Reckoning Collective
Edited By: Jessica Danger
Book Cover Art: Eve Von Bleyle
Book Cover Design: Tyler James Carroll

Printed in the United States of America

ISBN-13: 978-1-7376686-5-7 (paperback)

Dedication

To all the women who have held me together in love.

Bully

I have always known
The things that should be said,
But I learned to hold my tongue.
Fighting behind my teeth,
Angry energy
That found an outlet
Swinging at the world.
The only bully I can suffer
Is myself.

Army Brat

I left home so many times
I forgot where I was leaving
I grew up in 14 places
Many schools and temporary friends
But now I live in an old town
The kind of town
People's kids get stuck in
Where I watch my memories fade
Against unchanging architecture
I want to hold this mailing address
Longer than I've held any relationship
I want a home
Built on sidewalks where my friends
Used to live
But always come back
I want to be the one that stays
Somewhere
Anywhere
This time

Child Soldier

Before I could buy alcohol
I sold my innocence
For street cred in the brotherhood

I learned how to throw my hips
Into a punch
Before I understood
What my hips were for

I grieved a fallen soldier
Before I ever grieved a broken heart

Before I enjoyed the taste of coffee
And kisses
I enjoyed the taste of winning
And labored to hold it in my mouth

I fantasized about what it would be like to kill somebody
Before I thought to fantasize about marrying somebody

I knew the familiar taste of sweat
Crystallizing on my skin
Before I knew others would taste that way

I trained to carry the weight of a man
Before I had ever carried the weight of a man

Pre-Deployment Checklist

I don't know what the boys did.
We put on dresses
Or wife beaters
And went dancing.
Twirled in the parking lot
Until we puked.
We shared masturbation stories
In the ocean outside of Savannah
Then took pills to suppress our periods,
Flattened our boobs into body armor.
Restricting one need fed another.
While our friends back home
Shaved their curls for a night out,
We brought razors on deployment
And kept things trim,
Genuinely concerned about what the medics would say
If they had to cut our pants off.
We wrote death letters too,
Patriotism tinged with self-abandonment.
We
We are so few
Freaks until we met each other.

Non-Disclosure Agreement

Puffy red eyes
Over a drink
You told me I was a killer

You saw me
And said
There probably aren't many of us
But we are the same

You looked at me in mourning
The way I look at tigers in the zoo

For this reason
I will never tell your secrets
Or report your crimes

Even those against me

Amy Sexauer | Poppies

23

Portraits

They decorated their rooms
With wall-to-wall porn
Ten feet away the wall is decorated
With our dead.
Do the topless strangers
Make them feel more at home?
Or far enough away?
I am only numb beneath
All these eyes watching me.

22 October 2011

Sunlight glistens off the black polish
Of a graceful horse drawn carriage
How light is that casket they carry
They belong in a wedding parade
Not this procession of souls
That accompany her to the grave
Even in death, she is a light to be followed

Amy Sexauer | Poppies

Right of Bang (What Love Also Is)

What would be different
If I had been with you
That day
I still got your blood on my hands

Inventorying the bag full of shredded gear
We still hosed down the trucks
I still stacked up chow plates for everyone

Wrote reports
Signed statements
Held everyone's grief
And shared memories

I still called your Wife
And met your Mother
I still signed my name for yours
Over and over again
To clear you from base

I still recommended the medic for his medal
And held our team together
I know something is missing
But I don't know what I don't know

I didn't pull the trigger
Or tighten the tourniquet
But I was always there

Homecoming

I was there for nine months
We fought together for three
You trusted me
As one of the boys
If a quirky one.

I will never forget the look in your eyes
When I showed up in jeans,
Surrounded by other women at the bar
You realized I was one of them
Not one of you.

That night
I slept drunk
In the backseat
Of my car
Alone.

When Giants Fall

When giants fall
They fall hard.

Pull down mountains,
With their groping.

Crush cities and homes,
With their flailing.

There is no one left to mourn
When their shadows resolve to dust.

Conduct Unbecoming

Did you know
The challenges we would face
When you preached to us
About eyeliner
And the length of our shorts?

Show me how to lead humans
How to hold together many hearts
How to integrate the demons that will come.
Tell me how you broke
And put something back together.

Cowards
Do not lack bravery
But face the wrong threat.
You trapped us
Against the wrong enemy.

Black Beauty

I know what it's like
When angels come for you
Singing over the mountains
Black Beauty
Hope on rotors
They do not ride the wind
But create their own

My sister's first tattoo
Says that she will find a way or make one
As she levels a building

My other sister
Carries saints
Giving last rites
Tieing up loved ones
To bring home

I always smile and wave
When I hear the thrum over the horizon
Echos from my childhood

My dad smells like boot polish
And old flight hangers
He recognizes dead faces in the newspaper
He knows the sound of dog tags breaking
I know what they sound like
Snapping against my kit

Soldiers giving birth to soldiers
My father watches me
Fight the war of his youth
I ride in helicopters
But won't fly them

To say my family holds the sky
As we run beneath them
Is not poetic imagery

22 October 2012

Two embryos
Two heartbeats
Together from the moment
Cells divided
Twins
Separated by death
But connected by an umbilical cord
That can't be cut
Reaching through the thin membrane
That separates us from all we cannot hold
There are things
Only two hearts
Conceived together
Can know

Amy Sexauer | Poppies

Joy

I have known grief
That carries the gravity
Of a star
Into all moments
Leaving nothing else
To orbit

For every day
We have escaped
I celebrate my
Light feet
With dancing

Sisterhood

Barb mothered me
Eba mothered me
Laura mothered me
Jessie made me a big sister
Emily made me better

Caroline showed me faith
Tina showed me wit as a weapon
Liz showed me how to choose family over valor
Lizzy showed me light in dark places
Geneva showed me my independence is beautiful

Rachel taught me that women can possess beauty and other strengths
Alex taught me there is more to love than I learned in my childhood home
Shelane taught me how to listen to women
Lilia taught me you'll never regret being down for your friends
Aleah taught me how to be a soldier first

Meg is a courageous heart
Shanne is the best kind of friend
Andrea is the bravest woman I know
Kelly is a great mother
Kim is a guardian of gateways

Amy Sexauer | Poppies

Sexauer

My name has sex in it
So let's talk about it.

When I was four years old
I remember playground jokes
And knowing how to respond
Even when I didn't understand them.

In uniform
I watched every person
That shook my hand
Drag their eyes across my nametape;
I am fluent
In what their eyes are hiding.
Everyone flinches.

I made jokes and buried my sexuality.
I can build bridges between prudes and perverts.
Lauded for my humor and androgyny,
Now I hold cognitive dissonance.
Pride for my conduct most days,
But sometimes a sweet sadness
For the smothered youthful virility
That other soldiers are known for.

Brother

I refer to them
Collectively
And impersonally
As brothers
Brotherhood
Is a loaded term
For those oath takers
On the outside
But God gave me a blood brother
Who reminds me
There are good men
Outside of these rituals
I keep chasing

22 October 2013 (For Jennifer)

I wonder if your sisterhood beyond the grave
Is as strong as ours has become here
Same month
Same province
Same look in my friends' eyes
Grief is the bitter coffee
We continue to brew
How else to get out of bed
We can't bury another one
We keep burying another one
This garden we planted with our friends
Is eating itself

Same Bars

We went to the same bars
Young
And hungry for an inhibition
To match our adult responsibilities
I spun out of every grasp
Because I knew
If you knew
My job and rank
Your eyes would not be so bright
Honor is my fickle dance partner
Uptight they say
Even frigid
No
Just eager to be known
And wanted
Like everyone else

Platonic

You said you wanted to be my friend
Because I never finished an MRE
I was a virgin
And back then you kept count

You hooked up with my friends
And made me laugh
For the price of skittles
You taught me about innuendos
But I knew I was safe

Years later
At a chow hall overseas
There was pride in our eyes
As I told you all the ways I had grown up
And you had settled down

Me, learning to explore
A different side of men
While you,
Learned one woman
Longer than you had before

All for the price of skittles
A friend to mirror growth
A lesson in how
Some affections won't change
Even when we do

Amy Sexauer | Poppies

Deadline

The AC being out
Is supposed to deadline the vehicle
But if it rolls, it rolls.
Today, the engine still starts-
It doesn't matter
If everyone inside is roasting,
We'd do it for the bragging rights anyway,
Parading around in our sweat stains.
When the boss says
There will be a patrol
On this road 24/7
We have no choice
But to keep deadlined vehicles
Rolling out.

Amy Sexauer | Poppies

Sandstorms

I taste the sand
Before I see it.

Galloping along the horizon
Consuming leagues of desert
along with any expectations
Of what tomorrow might hold.

Anxiety is hungry for my time;
Tomorrow is already wasted.

Patches

A velcro patch
Doesn't make you legit
But my first one
I made with an exacto knife
Three crooked letters glowing in the dark
They sell them at the shoppette now

22 October 2014

When I die
I wonder if someone will
Put my name on their shorts
The girls and I
Ran a race together
In your honor
A fitting reunion
But is the flimsy silk
Bearing your name
And shifting in the wind
A fitting tribute
Your golden hair
Should be dancing in this wind
While we run

Amy Sexauer | Poppies

Amputee (Sam's Good Leg)

He told us it was easier to lose a leg
Than rehabilitate a shattered one

He wished they had just taken both

I wonder which parts of myself
I would rather amputate

Anger

I mix myself a drink
That will taste like anger
No matter the ratio
Of sadness and fear
I pour

Florence

I let myself cry tears
On the plane to Italy
Tried to take selfies
In burnt orange sunsets
Drank water from stone fountains
Smelled the familiar smell of piss
In the abandoned mountain sanctuary
Of a long dead monk
I needed Elizabeth Gilbert
And the smooth green marble of the Duomo
When I saw Michelangelo's David
I knew poetry was the language of angels
Attempting to imitate God

The Pines

We used to run
Over sandy trails
Underneath pine trees
That didn't smell like Christmas
Searching for affirmations
From our parents
That would never come
Begging our legs
To achieve things
Our hearts could not

22 October 2015

That time of year when you think it is summer
But then the mornings get hotter
Yellow pollen cooking on green wooden planks

Survivor's guilt is a hungry dog
Chasing my happy memories
Only the good die young
And I'm still here

Survivor's guilt doesn't care about our mothers
What would you go back and change?
Who would you protect from grief?
Those you couldn't protect with your death?

The shame matures with age
Wishing it had been me
Is less noble than it sounds

Amy Sexauer | Poppies

Pregnant

I told my company today that I'm pregnant
I'm in command of 77 human beings
And now they all know

I'm 30 years old
And still having sex with men that don't love me
Some mistakes have bigger consequences than others

No one loves a martyr
Unless you make them laugh
I made them laugh

While my world was falling apart
I used myself as a safety brief
And told them to learn from me

Amy Sexauer | Poppies

73

Kiss and Tell

We danced at my sister's wedding.
I thought, how could someone
Who touches my growing belly
And dances with me
Hate me so much?

It's not nice to kiss and tell
But it's hard to hide a baby.

The consequences of this heartbreak
Are my greatest achievements.

A rebirth,
A confidence in myself
I always pretended to have.

I know it wasn't me you hated.

Amy Sexauer | Poppies

Resilience

Resilience
Is not surviving,
Or enduring,
Or bouncing back.
It's crafting the story you need
From your ashes.
We are meaning makers.

Birth

God sat on my chest
And shoved coals down my throat
With a benevolent smile
While I raged
While I cried
While I begged

I felt no tenderness
But he held me anyway
As I choked on the smoke
As I coughed up the ashes of the old self
Hot coals rumbling around inside me

When I came to
There was a baby
Drinking nectar from my rotten chest
But she was not afraid of me

I reached down to touch
The stitches on my womb
And threw up my old heart
All over the hospital floor

Jyn

I'm throwing out
All my old journals
Filled with poems
About a melancholy heart
My heart was just waiting for you.

I'm learning so much about love
From getting on your level.
You don't care about the words
Or the wounds
You just want me to be here.

Getting to learn the world
All over again
Through your eyes
Is the sweetest
Benediction.

Amy Sexauer | Poppies

If I Didn't Have You

If I didn't have you
I would sleep more.
I might eat better.
I would have more time with my friends.
If I didn't have you,
I could spontaneously do
Whatever I wanted.
If I didn't have you
I would be making more money,
My life would be cleaner
And smoother,
If I didn't have you.

If I didn't have you,
I wouldn't be a mother.
I would still be lost,
And aimless
If I didn't have you.
I would still be looking for love
Outside of myself,
If I didn't have you.
I would laugh less
And sing less
And dance less
If I didn't have you.

If I didn't have you,
I'd have a whole lot of things
None of which compare
To you.

Amy Sexauer | Poppies

War Stories

I could tell my
Birth Story every day

Amongst mothers

It's the war story
That never gets old

22 October 2016

I can't remember a single word
Exchanged between us
Or even if these memories
Are mine
I've memorized all the photos
People continue to share
A whole woman
Reduced to the same five photographs
And a few whispers of energy
Stubbornly guarded
By those of us that were there
You drank the Holy Grail
And united us forever

Prayers

Today we prayed
At my kitchen table
I can't remember the last time
I let my prayers out of my mouth
As if my own ears would betray
My heart's desires
As if all my other senses
Can worship more innocently
Than my tongue

22 October 2017

Six years
Where have you been
I traveled around the world again
I loved and lost
I thought I loved then learned
I've shrunken from life
And regrown new parts
As the years continue to pass
My heart is heavy comparing
Our growing stories
With yours that ended too soon
Dreaming of where you could be
But I take comfort in knowing
That although you are unmoving
The place I'll always find you
Is right next to me

Arlington

I put on my sneakers
Packed water and sunscreen
To spend the day hiking
The nation's cemetery

How many football fields
Will it take to turn my stomach?

The neat manicured lawns
And precisely laid
Gravestones
Tucked into the evaporating
Landscape of our capital

The crosses at Normandy
Are the same shade of stone
But felt solemn

There are tourists at Normandy
But Arlington feels like a tourist attraction

One place feels consecrated
The other like a shiny facade
Designed to trap children

Poppies

We had to leave home for a time
In order to come home fully
Small wonder we chose to visit a graveyard
Nostalgic because it is far away
We don't know anyone buried there

A calm ocean and a soothing rain
Made space for our reflections
As we journeyed from beach to beach
Along France's northern border
Insulating our memories with history's heroes

The grass is neat and trim
Like the haircuts of young men
We climb over boulders
To find where it still grows
Long enough to dance in the wind

At Juno we joined
The anniversary celebrations
We felt communion
With the bright sprigs of red
Tucked within formal uniforms

Collars high, sleeves long
Buttons shined
Smooth and even
Rank and file ceremonies
No one here died so cleanly

Hidden beneath lapels
The poppy flower
Remembers
What it's like to grow wild
Before wilting in memoriam

They will wear her
Like a badge
They will crush her
To escape their pain
They will mold her
Into plastic

But generations
Of the fallen
Will welcome her home
Braided garlands of poppies
Weaved into their unshorn hair

I pray the dead are generous
With their symbols

Paris

Cobblestones here are older than my home
We came to visit the city liberated by our ancestors
And drank wine in Montemarte
Where Monet, Picasso, Renoir, and Van Gogh stayed
Now aspiring artists sell caricatures to tourists here
And we wonder what Kabul will look like in 70 years

Hindu Kush

The teeth of the Hindu Kush
Surround us
A tiny base
Sitting in the mouth
Of a laughing God

My own life feels significant
But all my aspirations
And potential
Are barely topsoil over the dregs
Of Empires past

Laid beneath
Another even layer
Of snow
Blanketing
Mountains

22 October 2018

The words don't come like they used to
But seven years later
I still shed tears for you
Holding my daughter in my arms
My heart has finally grown big enough
To wrap around this grief
And not try to manage it

Losing you
Is still
Devastating

Healthy Boundaries

Healthy
Boundaries
Are not just for
The innocent
Or the living

Peace Lily

The plant I bought yesterday
To make myself feel more nurturing;
A peace lily.
Already reaching
For the only light in this room
From a window carved into a door.
Leaves, like children's hands
Already reaching,
And one white blossom
Waving above them.

Green

The Hills of North Georgia
Shades of green

The sun's refining fire
Heating up

The stormy skies of summer
Make the air

Thick with nurturing rain and
Thick with memories I don't want

Can I find in these forests
More than the shades of greed and envy

Can I find the colors
of hope and growth?

22 October 2019

When we lost you
I wasn't yet a mother.

I thought I knew tragedy
But I was mourning rain drops.
You were someone's ocean
A mother who will forever look at the
World and see only desert.

Hogwarts

There is magic
In that bend of
The Hudson River
Granite stones wooed us
With the promise of
Being a part of history
Hallowed ground
Fed by generations
Of those too young
To place limits
On what they would sacrifice
The oaths we made with words
Differed from the ones
That grew in our hearts
Our battlefields
Would change
But our service
Would never falter

Note To Self

You could
Write an entire book
With the effort you are using
To avoid the story
You're supposed to write

Amy Sexauer | Poppies

22 October 2020

My dear friend
I'm always wondering if my memories
Are tricking me.

It's so strange to grow older
And carry you unchanged
In my heart forever.
Was our friendship what I still imagine it to be?
Do I have a right to grieve you even now?

Maybe in death, such insecurities
Don't matter.
You are an angel frozen in time,
Projecting blessings into this world
Through all that carry your glow.

Thank you.
Thank you.
Thank you.

Amy Sexauer | Poppies

All the Places I've Peed

When my pants were frozen because I had fallen into an icy river, I peed in order to thaw them. I sawed off the top of a Gatorade bottle and peed in the passenger seat of our moving HMMWV. In a Gatorade bottle in the back seat. So many Gatorade bottles. (None of said Gatorade bottles were thrown at civilians.) I've peed in a trash can. In porta potties under the watchful eye of dick drawings. In an Afghan kitchen because there was a drain. In the middle of a wide-open desert. I've peed incorrectly into a Thai squatty potty. In a specimen cup. In a specimen cup while someone watched. I peed in an outhouse on a hill where I could see the sky peeking through the hole in the ground. I've peed into a trough where I watched my waste merge into a stream. I've peed into a diaper. And my daughter's kiddie potty when she wouldn't get off the toilet. Behind a dumpster. Crouched behind an MRAP tire larger than me. In a catheter bag. Into a pad. At the Louvre. At the Vatican. In the Coliseum. A truckstop below the Great Wall. In the Gulf of Aqaba but not the Dead Sea. At least two oceans. All over my hand while trying to use a She-Wee. Into many wide mouthed beverage containers, usually in the back of my truck. On the side of many highways. Hovering over airport toilets. Crouching under my steering wheel at a National Park. When the infill was long and I didn't want to ask anyone to stop, I just peed my pants. I was sweaty anyway.

Amy Sexauer | Poppies

Failure

A baby falls down alot
While learning how to walk.

Mistakes and failures
Are simply the building blocks,
And to avoid the stumbling
Is to avoid the adventure.

Contradicting what I originally thought,
All my sins bring me closer to God.

Perspective

A perspective shift
At the end of things
The flat and muted browns of the desert
Set on fire by the setting sun
Vibrant purples, pinks, and oranges
Pulled from unexamined corners
That the sun, in its zenith,
Could not see

Slower

In this world
Of cultural ambiguity
We have created
Full of childhood wounds

There is nothing
We should assume
Even less left
To take for granted

The only remedy I know
For the lost
To find connection
Is to move slower

Intentional

Intentions are not ethics
Morality is a layer deeper
Than what you hope works out
How can virtues be anything less
Than ruthless?

Let's not just sort through our feelings
Let's tear them apart
We don't need naive saints
Nor ignorant sinners
We need warriors

Amy Sexauer | Poppies

22 October 2021

Ten years later and
We have insulated ourselves,
Turned shock and grief
Into calluses of the heart

A tree planted in your honor
Museum displays
Children named after you
Everyone pours out for you
In their own way

All I have are my words and
Ten years was too easy to count
But your legacy
Exponential through those that love you
Is immeasurable

Healers

I am sick
Of wounded healers
Sighing in ecstasy
As the tears of their patients
Soothe their own wounds

Independence

I resent
Blessings I didn't earn
I am suspicious
Of love that is easy

Amy Sexauer | Poppies

Green Chapel

This quilted blanket of forest
Green squares fading into blue
Who knew this bed
Could hold me
When the culture around
Its wildness
Was so suffocating
I didn't expect
To breathe easier here

Patterns

Managing chaos
Or dedicating yourself
To the control of things
That are not meant to be controlled

The best fighters
See patterns in the world
They've navigated internally
A million times before

Amy Sexauer | Poppies

Women Like Us

One day, someone will tell us
That we are the first
Or the only
So we feel special and
Isolated.

But history is full
Of women like us
And we are never
Alone.

Amy Sexauer | Poppies

Uniform

There are dresses in my closet
I'll never wear
Cut above the knee
With long sleeves
Backless
Nearly frontless
Rainbow sequins
All black
Some made for twirling
Some skin tight
I run my fingers over them
Before I grab
The boots I wear
Every day

Amy Sexauer | Poppies

Conifers

I creep beneath the conifers
Arrayed as fate would have them
Allowing bushes to grow
In the cracks of sunlight
That break through their canopies

In my front yard
There is a large solitary oak
Nothing can grow
Beneath it's shade

My best gifts are observations
I have never created anything new

On Wisteria

The cadence of my feet
As I run into twilight
Embraced by the scent
Of wisteria
Carried on the humidity
Latent all year
Unseen she climbs the tallest trees
To explode in spring
Purple highlights at every street corner
The perfume in the warm air
Makes me feel like a woman

Desire

Latitude lines
Measure where the sun
Is nourishing or burning
Desire
Breaks over the horizon
After a long night
Thawing skin
Itching for a sunburn
Not soft like
The insubstantial curves of a cloud
But soft like the stones
Worn smooth beneath a river
By eons of gentle friction
The sun is eons old
But for us
Those fractured colors of sunrise
Renew each morning

Amy Sexauer | Poppies

Plans

I stopped asking God
For anything.
I hold gratitude like my daughter
In my arms every night.
I stopped begging the universe
To take it easy on me.
The things I always wanted
Are no longer for me.

COLLECTIVE

DEAD RECKONING COLLECTIVE is a veteran owned and operated publishing company. Our mission encourages literacy as a component of a positive lifestyle. Although DRC only publishes the written work of military veterans, the intention of closing the divide between civilians and veterans is held in the highest regard. By sharing these stories it is our hope that we can help to clarify how veterans should be viewed by the public and how veterans should view themselves.

Visit us at:

deadreckoningco.com

@deadreckoningcollective

@deadreckoningco

@DRCpublishing

Follow Amy Sexauer

 @amyontap

AMY SEXAUER is a poet hailing from a dozen different military bases around the world. After being raised in a military family, she spent nine years on active duty and is now serving in the U.S. Army Reserves. She manages a small charity in Southern Pines, North Carolina where she lives with her daughter and two dogs.

CPSIA information can be obtained
at www.ICGtesting.com
Printed in the USA
BVHW030853151221
624107BV00007B/238